Grace Clancy is a young woman with a passion for poetry and feels words have a powerful existence in the world. She was born and raised in a small town surrounded by loved ones she holds dear to her heart. She continues to find joy in the little things in life through every moment.

To the feelings that make us whole.

Grace Clancy

THE HARDEST PART

AUSTIN MACAULEY PUBLISHERS™

LONDON · CAMBRIDGE · NEW YORK · SHARJAH

Ordering Information
Quantity sales: Special discounts are available on quantity purchases by corporations, associations, and others. For details, contact the publisher at the address below.

Publisher's Cataloging-in-Publication data
Clancy, Grace
The Hardest Part

ISBN 9798889105350 (Paperback)
ISBN 9798889105862 (ePub e-book)

Library of Congress Control Number: 2023920556

www.austinmacauley.com/us

First Published 2024
Austin Macauley Publishers LLC
40 Wall Street, 33rd Floor, Suite 3302
New York, NY 10005
USA

mail-usa@austinmacauley.com
+1 (646) 5125767

Thank you to my mother, who always supported me and encouraged my creativity as a child. I've grown to be a strong woman under her wing, and this book would not be possible without her.

A child from heaven is still just a child
scream all you want
she's still gonna cry
give her a while
and she'll still be just a child
wide-eyed
and innocent
you don't trust her
heaven sent
she was hand-crafted to lie
right to your face
and isn't it so confusing
to hold so much in your hands
the whole world
but only as it crumbles
and falls apart in your gaze
she was just a phase.

A place to sit
and lay with my thoughts
my sanctuary
so hard to leave
and easy to love
my world goes dark
an endless cove,
until I hit rock bottom
one more leap to never land
hold my hand for one more high
for one more time
deja vu
me and you
we dance in the dark
until you eat me alive
and I don't say a word
consumed by the comfort.

A sunset I won't forget
a long talk I'll soon regret
with my eyes closed, we might see
you speak with your back turned to me
my life's in pieces on the floor,
I'm addicted to the way my eyes feel sore
when I look at your face and beg for more.

All I could ask for
leave my mind
nevermore
I talk to you at night
close my eyes in the sun
forevermore
I'll never understand how I got here
under the warmth
I won't remember you
buried in the earth
I'll suffocate before I open my eyes
I don't trust you.

And here I am
every breath I take
every word I speak
heart I break
and dream I chase
I'll take advantage of it
the existence in more worlds than one
every version of me sees through these eyes
it's different every time
and my chances to see the sun will bleed me dry
pain, I can only dream of.

At the end of every day
lost in my thoughts
I can't even stand up
too much silence
just to end the night with violence
my brain stops,
and I can't think of a word to describe the feeling
I'm trapped
and left reeling
in utter awe of how far behind I can fall
when counting my moments of success
I've come so far
just to feel the same
every face I blame
when a moment becomes just a blur well spent.

By the light of the moon
begging for a chance
I wish I didn't wish I was different
breaking down towers of resentment
I don't have the guts to look at you
your eyes make me nervous,
you'll kiss me in the rain
with feelings we'd rather not discuss
I'll see you again.

Caught off guard
if only I could have lived better
so much potential for a person
filled with pity
and plenty of things to do
everything to feel and nothing to lose
fight for so long for a chance
to look in the mirror with pride
you'll cry for everyone,
because you can't quite get enough
and put yourself through some more,
you're hurt and it shows
try for a disguise
to match the motions you go through,
tired of fighting
just to feel something.

Consumed by the moments I can't let go
you sing to me the whole way home
you're nice for the moment,
naive in every sequence
this high is too frequent
annoyed,
I've heard this song before
I won't tell you
and you won't leave me
I leave it be.

Devastated to dance more dances
read the room
and it's hard to breathe
there's no room to dance
it's demanding
stranded by the lights
it's demeaning
I don't think it was meant to get this far
just close enough
I can't tell
just a feeling.

Eventually
it sits on your mind
and plants a garden in your soul
you love the flowers
therefore, you must love the rain.

Everything just blends together
people pleaser
treat it all the same
you have a problem,
can't tell the difference
when it's survival of the fittest.

Find the guts to show some emotion
this is it
born to live and made to die
cause a commotion,
the ringing in my ears that won't go away
I try to listen
but it's not that simple, is it
to read between the lines
and reach your great fulfillment
you are just your parents
just fluent in the motion of one day at a time
but it's still just too much
towers of guilt
too cold to care for
I don't know if I'm a good person anymore
and it makes me sick to my stomach to feel it.

Finding forgiveness
I released my grip on life
but I wish it meant something
I'm forever chasing an idea
of a meaningful day
a likable person
a lovable daughter
I hold on to the person I'm expected to be
yet, I don't have the heart to wait for her
it's meaningless
when there's no tomorrow.

Forced myself to leave my skin
and crawl back home
left and right the golden sin
where do I begin
a story of a God who won't count the leaves as they fall
but I'll count every tear that falls from your face
everyone might,
left to wonder what's right
and tell you you're wrong,
listen to the right song
and call it a night
every winter you're lost
just in the moment
and you praise the heart
that melts in your hands
you lost your mind to play the part
you sing me a song
and I pretend I don't exist
we can dance all day
and close our eyes
when we cross paths at night.

Fridays start to feel like Saturdays
I'll pray for you in the month of May
I only wish you could have stayed
I can't change my mind, I'll stay at bay
built to sway
rewrite my story, call it luck
I'll fantasize until I die
about a dream that isn't mine
close the doors and feel the breeze of time,
we'll meet again another time
in between my dreams
I'll see your face, it's written in the seams
wrapped around my heartstrings
in my head every thought that stings
I hold you so close to me
my bittersweet memory.

I can feel it
the heat on my skin
anger seems to fit
just feel it
and wait for her to speak
it's almost too much
you're cold and you can't breathe
wait for it
we're all just bones underneath.

I can still taste it
love on the tip of my tongue
bitter
it soaked my eyes as I stared you up and down
left me with thoughts I can't bother to dance around
I look at you but you can't see it
it's on the tip of your tongue
isn't she so young
to be so lovable
I can hardly stand it
the way you stare
and I can hardly handle the moves you make
just to see me
my endless pit of excuses
you dig the hole just a little bit deeper
anything to keep her.

I can't handle change
not the way I used to
I'm not the same
but my guilt stays
in a way I'm not used to
life is more than just a dream to me,
I chase your idea of me
I mull over the question
of who I'm meant to be
I could scream for hours
a bloody shower
peel my eyes from my face
and call it a disgrace
embrace the loss of love
after the storm,
I can't retrace
where I went wrong.

I don't even have it in me to cry
force myself to forget your name,
my face is covered in your agony
I'll try again one day
shed a tear for every moment beyond me
and every time I wish I was different
the same song plays when I scream your name
but you won't listen
and the way your eyes glisten
almost makes this easy.

I don't dance with the devil
we talk amongst the morning
I tell him I wanted things to be different
and he tells me God wanted it this way,
that maybe I should appreciate the moment he gave me
I hold my tongue,
he'll never ask for my hand
he'll never ask for one song
but he'll listen and never tell me I'm wrong,
gives me everything I want, he knows I've earned it
God will brush my hair
and tell me I'm pretty despite it
but the devil and I are close knit
we cross paths
but we don't dance
I'm never invited.

I don't know when to walk away
I just know when I want to
and I don't think I'll kiss you goodnight
you won't fight,
my reflection in the puddle
I'm a mess
you can't ignore
so you adore it
I don't think I like this anymore.

I don't like the way you look at me anymore
it's too similar to the way I look at myself
I wanna love you but I don't know how
somehow, I'm not convinced I can
chase me in your dreams
wherever I land
your reflection is yours
as is mine
you won't listen to the rain
you just give it some time.

I face you in the moment
but never, it seems
sick with envy
I can't be bothered to chase my dreams
but I'll still be here at the end of the day
an endless wait for things to change
one more hour, my mouth goes sour
an awkward stance, a feeling so strange
I'm still in bed, maybe a problem, perhaps
because the sheets aren't comfortable anymore,
in fact I picture them a new shade
I can't outrun the relapse
a time trap
left to decay.

I feel nothing, but when I look at you
my soul looms empty as your eyes fill me up
my time with you can't replace everything I've lost
but even for a second, it makes me feel
and that's all I long for
to feel something in this world so blue
and every time I find my something in you.

I feel so out of place
but I fit in your arms just right
it was nice
even if it wasn't the right place
just the look on your face
could make me question the moon
maybe even the stars
the way the sun rises
and why it falls
but it was nice
the way I knew I loved you
just a feeling
and no questions at all
how ornate
you love the dance
but only when it's late
you love me, you think you might,
the same way you chase the sunset
so close
but not quite.

I get up just to sit and ponder
I can't let my mind wonder
a blank page I can't fill
no time to kill
trapped in my thoughts and feelings
I don't think I'll escape
because maybe I'm tired of trying
a fear of free falling
with no fear of dying.

I hate nighttime
I never shut up
too tired to convince myself I'm fine
stuff my face with thoughts that don't exist
you never shut up
make myself sick with the idea that you love me
you find it funny,
you make me sick
I'll throw it up to make you proud
the fantasy
lay it on the ground
try to avoid the crowd
that crawls under my skin
holds my breath hostage
kills my peace of mind.

I just wish you thought of something else when you looked
at me
but just take whatever you want
who cares
if that's all I am
I can't look people in the eyes
gross
I can't even get close
covered in the shame
I'm drenched
I can't find a moment where I don't regret it
I can't forget it
I was used
and it plays on repeat on my mind every day
I'm more than just a body
but only to me it seems
the child in me screams
just for a moment to breathe.

I never needed to have it all
I just asked for some silence
and they told me to be quiet,
you'll cry about it
the fact I turned out this way
but my eyes are open
and I'm not sure what's worse
to be hurt
or to be the curse
how absurd
I'm on the outskirts of insanity.

I wish I didn't care so much
and I wish you didn't hold my hand so tight
I wish you could read my mind,
I wish you didn't talk so much
and I wish this felt right
you make me uneasy
it was too easy
for you to look me in the eyes
and think to yourself that this is alright
I was too young to know your mom
too young to drink
too young to drive
I didn't know the answer
I didn't even know the question
awestruck
what did you think when you saw her
just my luck.

I'll be ready
when the right wave comes
I'll feel the warm breeze on my face
and the soft sand underneath
I'll be here waiting
because now the tides stay low, scared to surface
but when the wave comes, I'll take it all in at once
as its confidence leaves me starstruck.

I'll tear myself apart
just to get you to look at me
rip my skin off
and tie it in a bow
a glance is all I need
I'll spell it out with my blood
just to get you to understand
I love you, with a passion
just enough you demand
your uncanny resemblance to the devil
just for you I'll dance till I'm tired
my bones crumble at your desire
stippling marks of unchecked boxes
hearts in lockets
on your hands, my lipstick
I'm a disaster of emotion
tucked inside your pocket.

If I could take it all back
treat myself better
change your perspective
lost in chaos
I'll meet your eyes
treat it as loss
I suppose it's just the rain
that'll make this more than enough
forget who I am
I dispose my attention
a misinterpretation of a perfect connection.

In a parallel universe, we look the same
but we feel different
you look at me longer
and think of me frequent
I'm so glad I met you
if only it meant something.

In due time
you'll stay mine
the sun will still rise and stand tall
even when you give it your all
we're free to jump
as were free to fall
I'll be gone and so will the stars in the day
but to exist in this world
as an old soul, ruthless and tired, I'll never stay
because I can't be bothered to test the waters
surrounded by sons and daughters
the ocean will tell a story about us
with words I could never say
you loved this life
and I loved you
with your eyes closed
standing in the sand
I was there, a simple breeze
I held your hand,
and for once we breathed with ease.

It's just a dream I had in mind
to leave
and settle in a new place I find
I do believe
I'm not supposed to be here
It's a trap
in constant fear
a misguided perhaps
of poems in a fucking bathroom
and a stupid costume
it's a dumb facade
come a little closer
see the mush of the unflawed
my mind's abroad
don't just whisper
tell her you're a fraud
yell at her in black and white,
keep it risqué
and leave her to dance in the gray.

Keep my heart level on the shelf
at the end of the day it's all about control
I shift my weight
try to feel whole
try to feed my soul
never enough
I'll see the light of day
I can't have it either way
but I'll never rest
till I see your face
because you take me as naive
and my rampage is a color I can't perceive
painted behind my eyes
you're an artist at heart
I'll let you tear me apart
eat me alive
moments I learn to despise
as I long for the day where remorse is a memory
of you and me
I'll never be free
you, only I can see
you, a simple reflection of me.

Life's in waves
on the shore
most at night, knocking on my door
I always answer because it's not fair
I can't help but wonder who's there
I face you in the moment but never it seems
but once the sun rises, a knock is still at my door
because life still comes in waves
but sometimes we hide it.

Maybe I just don't understand
filled with shame
I can't handle the moment
it makes me sick
to think of you
give me a taste of love
just a lick
from an angel-shaped spoon
sprinkled like dust
nicknamed lust
break my heart I dare you,
even if you cared to
my bags are packed
the glass is cracked
and you still can't see me the same.

My memories of late nights
restless in the sheets my mind won't stop
running through the flashing lights
of every moment I can never forget
one more thing hanging over your head
that feeling you've met
you can't remember the name.

My mind is so foggy
I can't remember the day
it bothers me to try
eat one more meal
tell one more lie
but you aren't quite satisfied
your washed-up emotions turn your thoughts to mush
but you don't have much,
the end of every day is just night
but that doesn't quite sit right with you,
your upturned stomach
and your fraction of innate comprehension
too much tension on the brain
I'll throw up
and I'll cry
and I'll spit on the floor if I please,
if it brings down some ease.

My past self comes back just to remind me I hate myself
never good enough
maybe I messed up
maybe I'm anxious
fighting for some peace
maybe if I say please
thank you
let me beg you
on this dirty floor
if this was a mistake
then this must be the place.

No matter how hard I lie
the birds will still fly
to be precious is the old way to qualify
for a sweet life
in a blind testimony
I'll notify the angel from my shoulder
to take it easy
as she sleeps on my chest,
lessons learned at best
my rampage is over
now I must rest.

Perhaps it was all a dream
a silly scheme
illuminated as the moon beams
my life in pieces, it glistens
no one ever listens
when you relapse
my tears fall one after the other
an endless stream
you seem
unfazed by the mess
you seem to ignore it.

Read between my lines
I left the door open to leave
my face goes red, you can't read me
I'm left alone
one step away
leave me alone
everywhere I turn
your smell lingers
everywhere I find
the stain of your fingers
all over my body
and the fine lines of my mind.

Reconcile the silence
anything for you
just to break apart my whispers
you'd be someone to look up to
but your eyes are too blue
and under the influence
you sit in my mind
waiting for your moment
the perfect timing
when you're free to roam
the space is yours
and the silence is daunting
you might as well haunt me
the way I don't feel the moments
I fantasize
my heartbeat against your chest
I get butterflies, the way we dance in the dark.

Remember where you lay
you're delicate
and it's written on your face
these are your words
of despair
and misery
your book of poems you wrote for me
signed by the insanity
every debt you pay
just call me yesterday
and don't think of me tomorrow
because I dreamt of you tonight.

Room full of stars
I open the window
because I'm not scared to die,
to do as I'm told
I'll let them in
and set the world on fire because I'm cold
I'm scared I'll never be warm again
it's too much to think about
the way the stars burn at a distance
the way no one knows the difference.

Seasick
on my own
my thoughts twist and turn
your face makes my stomach tighten
the knots in my body
what I see makes me sick
it's so easy to forget you
cherry cheeks
call me just to forget
to remember me when you wake up.

Some simple stance on life
how I see things with my eyes closed
and how I touch the dirt with my hands to feel close to home
on my own I'll grow
but I can't speak a sentence to you
the days I go through
I can't remember your name
the clouds in my mind make it hard to understand
I can't recognize the way the rain makes me feel
this can't be real
irritated, I have more cards to deal
and you have your poker face
hidden underneath my dress
one day I'll learn to love you less
when I can find the sun in my mind again.

Sometimes I feel like giving a bullshit answer
because I think it will make things end better
I'm not a liar
I just think of the future too much
and how you'll always be better off
knowing nothing about me
but you step too close to the sun
and cry for the moon
maybe I'm just having fun
but last night I knew you
today I don't
saboteur
I labeled you,
led astray
I lost you in the memory
but not the moment.

The art of dancing in the rain
painting guilt on my face
and screaming till I empty my veins
the clouds have never moved so fast
so many conversations at once
I'll let every word pass
my mind races through the moments
of unrequited emotion
your stippling devotion
to never looking me in the eyes
and filling my memory with actions I despise
too close of a call
I can feel it all
the raindrops on my skin
an ever-lasting, never dying sin
to just enjoy the rain.

The idea that the devil dances
still sits on my mind
I'm annoyed
so many chances to change
the veins in my hands are too blue
and I can't stop shaking
I can't stop thinking
I leave you on the dance floor
but you still want more
it's a good thing the devil dances,
his own image of love
is counting my footsteps as I walk away
a tease
you don't understand
he doesn't dance to please
it's almost over.

The loveliest lies
whisper sweet words to me
and walk with grace and disguise
in a manner of innocent compliance,
savory with a smile
stay for a while.

The moment of clarity comes when you least expect it
simple silence
you walk through the storm and somehow find yourself in
the eye of it
out of nowhere the fog is gone
a whisper that says go on
and in the corner sits a black swan
the switch from a devotee
divine timing leads a revolt I cannot see,
and dream to be wrong
as the birds cry a screech in song
I'm covered in the rain
unfamiliar in the pattern of a bloodstain.

Wait till sunrise
to beg me for the sunset
don't give into it
the colors hurt your eyes
you can't get enough
how did you end up so rough
around all your edges
easy
with the control you let free
don't get lost inside a hole you can't fill
those emotions you let in
won't leave you flowers
they can tell you're just a coward.

Walking backwards
to live in chaos
I'll find peace later
and differentiate the silence after the rain
from when you wish you've had enough.

We dance to the color green
pleased to meet you
it burns
and my face feels hot
my heartbeat matches the song
and your eyes match the sky
the indifference I go through
I just wish I knew what to say to you
the feeling hovers
you mean more to me than I thought
my unforeseen lover
somewhere with you
I can only dream to be
maybe if I had only done things differently
I feel the way you look at me
those feelings you hid
you have no idea who I am
you wouldn't look at me the same if you did.

When I watch the last tear
fall from your cheek
I'll realize my dreams were flooded with the idea of you
and how you felt
you aren't forever, you never were
so when you left, all I had was me
and a pile of dreams that were nevermore.

Yesterday felt like a fever dream
I'm sick with envy
I'll scream for hours
as the memories become deadly
the reminiscence is a relapse
and I'll watch my life collapse
when my words get stuck in my throat,
I never learned to talk to you
only listen to every word you wrote
till my knees feel the drop
and my hands hit the floor
I'll crawl to every corner just to reach the top
I can't remember where you were or how we met
all I know is that we did
and the thought of you is fuzzy
but the feeling makes me wish you could have known
I was just a kid.

You always needed more than me
undo your name on my skin
because you always wanted more
I was never enough
just enough
someone to listen
someone to sleep with
I couldn't even utter a word
tell you to stop
you needed more
and I never had the courage to stop you from taking it
I was never enough of a person to tell you I'm too young
you wouldn't listen if I did
a pretty face has nothing important to say
not when your hands were already on me
you took everything
ripped my innocence out of my body
I was just anybody
now I can never take enough showers
with all my power
I still can't forgive myself
for what you did to me.

You don't know how to act
just like you don't know how to say no
one breath at a time
when my stomach hurts
when your lips meet mine
when I'm nauseous
when we're intertwined
just an idea
maybe a dream we had in mind
we've been here before
I couldn't breathe either time.

You don't know where you're going
all you know is where you've been
it'll make your heart burst
the thought of where to begin
you close your eyes as you walk past the mirror
because you can't help but miss her
you feel closer
you've come so far
just to crumble
when you're reminded of who you actually are.

You didn't know me
you knew the grief
and you can almost feel the way I'm too tired
to even look at you
I don't care about what I was supposed to do
daydreaming
I only knew the anger
this will only pass through.

You feel bad about who you are
try to visualize
a better life,
can't fight the feeling
can't even face it,
big on love
and how it left you hanging
just erase it
it could be that easy
if you just remembered who you are
and how your life has changed.

You see it now
there is no way life is meant to be felt
and there is no way to deal with the rain
the tears as they come
and even as they go
feel it
and give them a show
of the divine
and all that's fine in the world
everything the sun will touch
after it all
you won't remember me
and I won't forget you
my beach baby
my one true love
my reflection during the day
and your reflection at night
the way you smile at me
the way you know me so well.

You sit and watch the time tick by
then scream about how it's all going too fast
take it all in
the sun will still set when your dead
and the moon will shine on your bed sheets
the dust will settle and time will still tick by
even though you take it all in one day at a time
just one more second
maybe you'll do right this time,
maybe not
or you won't do it at all
you can't focus hard enough to realize,
time isn't your biggest fear
it's just the feeling.

You'll always take it farther than everyone else
and when the planets collide
I'm scared to feel remorse for the woman I could have been
all just for a little but of love
tired of the things that make me feel alive
you think about it
often
knowing the answer.

You're just overwhelmed
by the mess
by the reflection
by every test
one more and then you're done
followed by another
I didn't think you could love so much
and still be disappointed by her
the person you grew to be
the silence followed by an overture
is the melody of broken furniture
and the hate you have for her.